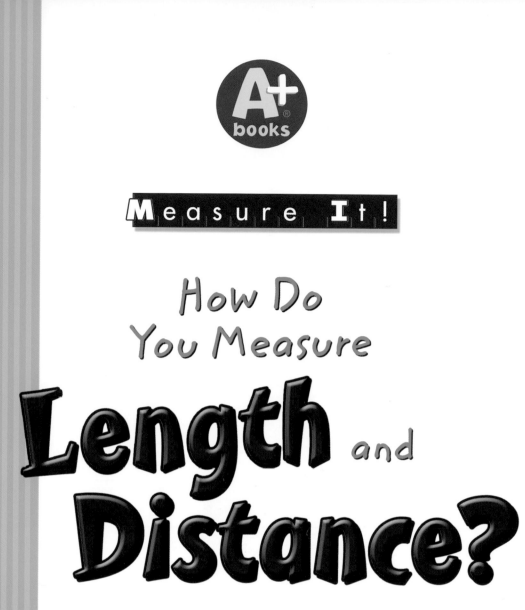

A+ books

Measure It!

How Do You Measure
Length and Distance?

by Thomas K. and
Heather Adamson

CAPSTONE PRESS
a capstone imprint

Sue's flower is growing.

How tall is it? How can she tell?
She needs a way to measure.

Is it the size of her foot?
No, her foot is too big.

Is it the size of her nose?
No, her nose is too small.

3

Is the flower
the size of
her hand?

Yes, that works.

But wait.

Hands come in all sizes. "One hand tall" means something different when we use someone else's hand. What should Sue do?

You can use anything to measure, including your hand. But people have made <u>standard tools</u> to help everyone measure the same way.

Rulers, yardsticks, and tape measures are tools.

They measure how long, how tall, how far, or how deep.

metal tape measure

yardstick

cloth
tape measure

ruler

People use inches, feet, and yards to measure how long, how tall, or how deep. Place the zero end of a tool at one end of an object. Then find the number at the other end. This number is the measurement.

One Yard   1|8   1|4   3|8

zero end

The metric system uses centimeters, meters, and kilometers to measure how long, how tall, or how deep. In this book, metric measurements are shown in parentheses next to the other measurements.

measurement

Let's measure Sue's plant in inches.

We're measuring height. That's how tall something is.

The ruler shows that her plant is 5.5 inches (14 centimeters) tall.

What else can we measure?

How about Gary the guinea pig? Instead of his height, we'll measure how long he is, or his length.

The ruler shows he's 7 inches (17.8 cm) long.

What's longer than Gary?

Let's check Barney the dog.
He's longer than one ruler.
It's time to measure with feet.
But not Sue's feet!

One ruler is 1 foot (0.3 meter).
One yardstick is 3 feet,
or 1 yard (0.9 m).

The dog is 2 feet (0.6 m) long.

Barney is longer than three Garys!

How long is the bed?

Sue needs two yardsticks to measure it.
The bed is 2 yards, or 6 feet (1.8 m), long.

Barney!
Off the bed.

What's longer than the bed?

Sue goes out to the garage. The truck looks pretty long. What tool could she use to measure it?

She'll use a tape measure.
The truck is 16 feet (4.9 m) long.

Sue's dad says it's time to leave.
How far will they go?
Long distances are measured in miles. A car can count the number of miles it travels.

60

40

80

20

100

P
R
N
D
S

ODO

660

120

km/h

MPH

start trip

The trip is 5 miles (8 kilometers) from Sue's house.

They went to the pool!

Water is measured in depth, or the height from the surface downward.

The water in the pool is 3 feet (0.9 m) deep. Will the water be over Sue's head?

We can measure her height to check. Remember that the yardstick is 3 feet. Is Sue taller than the water is deep?

Yes, she is.
Time to swim!

There are many ways to measure
length, distance, height, and depth.
All you need is the right tool.

Sue and her flower
keep getting taller.

How tall will
they grow?

Cool Measuring Facts

• As of 2009, the tallest dog in the world is a Great Dane. Titan is 42.25 inches (107.3 cm) from the bottom of his paw to his shoulder.

a Great Dane

• The world's longest goldfish measured 18.7 inches (47.5 cm).

- The world's tallest sunflower was measured at 25 feet, 5.4 inches (7.8 m) in the Netherlands.

- A redwood in California is the world's tallest living tree, at 378.1 feet (115.2 m).

- As of 2009, the world's tallest man is Sultan Kosen, at 8 feet, 1 inch (246.4 cm).

- A woman named Xie Quiping from China has the world's longest hair. In 2004, it measured 18 feet, 5.54 inches (5.63 m).

Glossary

depth—the height of something as measured from a surface downward; pools are measured in depth

distance—how far it is from one point to another

foot—a unit of length that equals 12 inches

height—how tall something is

inch—a unit of length; there are 12 inches in a foot

length—how long something is

measure—to find out the size of something

metric system—a system of measurement based on counting by 10s; meters and kilometers are basic units of measuring length in the metric system

mile—a unit of length equal to 5,280 feet

ruler—a long, flat piece of wood, metal, or plastic used for measuring length; rulers are usually 1 foot in length

tape measure—a measuring device made of a long piece of ribbon or metal that rolls out

yard—a unit of length equal to 3 feet

yardstick—a stick used to measure length that is one yard, or 3 feet, long

Read More

Anderson, Jill. *Measuring with Sebastian Pig and Friends: On a Road Trip.* Math Fun with Sebastian Pig and Friends! Berkeley Heights, N.J.: Enslow Publishers, 2009.

Marrewa, Jennifer. *Measuring on a Treasure Hunt.* Math in Our World, Level 2. Pleasantville, N.Y.: Weekly Reader Pub., 2008.

Roy, Jennifer Rozines, and Gregory Roy. *Measuring at Home.* Math All Around. New York: Marshall Cavendish Benchmark, 2007.

Internet Sites

FactHound offers a safe, fun way to find Internet sites related to this book. All of the sites on FactHound have been researched by our staff.

Here's all you do:

Visit *www.facthound.com*

Type in this code: 9781429644563

Index

A+ Books are published by Capstone Press,
151 Good Counsel Drive, P.O. Box 669, Mankato, Minnesota 56002.
www.capstonepub.com

Printed in the United States of America in North Mankato, Minnesota.
112010
006003R

Books published by Capstone Press are manufactured with
paper containing at least 10 percent post-consumer waste.

Library of Congress Cataloging-in-Publication Data
Adamson, Thomas K., 1970–
  How do you measure length and distance? / by Thomas K. and
Heather Adamson.
    p. cm. – (A+ books. Measure it!)
  Summary: "Simple text and color photographs describe the
units and tools used to measure length and distance"—Provided
by publisher.
  Includes bibliographical references.
  ISBN 978-1-4296-4456-3 (library binding)
  ISBN 978-1-4296-6330-4 (paperback)
  1. Length measurement—Juvenile literature. 2. Units of
measurement—Juvenile literature. I. Adamson, Heather, 1974–
II. Title. III. Series.
  QC102.A33 2011
  530.8'1—dc22   2010002811

Credits
Gillia Olson, editor; Juliette Peters, designer; Sarah Schuette,
    photo studio specialist; Marcy Morin, studio scheduler;
    Laura Manthe, production specialist

Photo Credits
All photos by Capstone Studio/Karon Dubke

Note to Parents, Teachers, and Librarians
The Measure It! series uses color photographs and a nonfiction
format to introduce readers to measuring concepts. *How Do
You Measure Length and Distance?* is designed to be read
aloud to a pre-reader, or to be read independently by an early
reader. Images and narrative promote mathematical thinking by
showing that objects and time have measurable properties, that
comparisons such as longer or shorter can be made between
multiple objects and time-spans, and that there are standard
and non-standard units for measuring. The book encourages
further learning by including the following sections: Cool Facts,
Glossary, Read More, Internet Sites, and Index. Early readers
may need assistance using these features.